happy birthday to you

28016857R00059

Printed in Great Britain
by Amazon